CANADA AND THE UNITED STATES

EDITED BY NICK WINNICK

Weigl

CALGARY
www.weigl.com

Published by Weigl Educational Publishers Limited
6325 10 Street SE
Calgary, Alberta, Canada
T2H 2Z9

Website: www.weigl.com
Copyright ©2009 WEIGL EDUCATIONAL PUBLISHERS LIMITED
All rights reserved. No part of this publication may be reproduced, stored in a retrieval system, or transmitted in any form or by any means, electronic, mechanical, photocopying, recording, or otherwise, without the prior written permission of the publisher.

Library and Archives Canada Cataloguing in Publication data available upon request.
Fax (403) 233-7769 for the attention of the Publishing Records department.

ISBN 978-1-55388-488-0 (hard cover)
ISBN 978-1-55388-489-7 (soft cover)

Printed in the United States of America
1 2 3 4 5 6 7 8 9 0   12 11 10 09 08

All of the Internet URLs given in the book were valid at the time of publication. However, due to the dynamic nature of the Internet, some addresses may have changed, or sites may have ceased to exist since publication. While the author and publisher regret any inconvenience this may cause readers, no responsibility for any such changes can be accepted by either the author or the publisher.

Weigl acknowledges Getty Images as its primary image supplier for this title.
Other credits include: Library and Archives of Canada: page 44 bottom right; MODIS Rapid Response Team, NASA Goddard Space Flight Center Images captured by the MODIS instrument on board the Terra or Aqua satellite: page 20 top.

Every reasonable effort has been made to trace ownership and to obtain permission to reprint copyright material. The publishers would be pleased to have any errors or omissions brought to their attention so that they may be corrected in subsequent printings.

We acknowledge the financial support of the Government of Canada through the Book Publishing Industry Development Program (BPIDP) for our publishing activities.

EDITOR: Heather C. Hudak
DESIGN: Terry Paulhus

Canada and the United States
Contents

Canada and the United States Through the Years	4
2000s	6
1990s	10
1980s	14
1970s	18
1960s	22
1950s	26
1940s	30
1930s	34
1920s	38
1910s	42
1900s	44
Activity	46
Further Research	47
Glossary/Index	48

Canada and the United States
Through The Years

Throughout history, Canada and the United States have worked together in many ways. These two nations have aided in conflict resolution across the globe, been instrumental in encouraging peace agreements between warring nations, and provided relief for struggling countries. As two of the most powerful nations in the world, Canada and the United States are able to use their influence to guide other countries through difficult times and offer assistance in the form of funds, military action, and mediation.

The United States and Canada are both powerful nations. They have vast natural resources and access to advanced technology. However, to ensure these nation remain respected leaders, they must find ways to successfully work and communicate with each other.

Since the first European explorers arrived in what is now North America hundreds of years ago, Canada has had military, economic, and cultural relationships with the United States. In the 20th century, both nations have been a major influence in a number of global issues. Together, Canada and the United States have experienced great struggles and incredible successes. Through it all, they have continued to be dedicated to the ideals of democracy, freedom, and justice.

In the years to come, Canada and the United States will face many new challenges and opportunities. Climate change, dwindling resources, and political instability are just a few of the issues taking shape as we move deeper into the 21st century. Throughout history, these two nations have proven that they can aptly adjust to and persevere in any new situation.

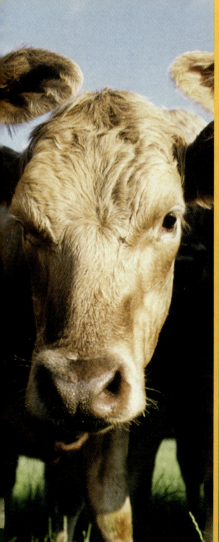

Canada and the United States
2000s

2000s

Standing Alone

In 2001, the United States was attacked by terrorists. Responsibility for the attack lay with a group called al-Qaeda. Many members of this group were tracked to Afghanistan, where they were receiving support from the government. The United States organized a counterattack against al-Qaeda and its allies in Afghanistan, called the Taliban. Many nations, including Canada, aided the United States in this effort. A number of al-Qaeda terrorists were captured or killed, and the Taliban government was toppled. Canada, the United States, Great Britain, France, and other nations continue the effort to stabilize Afghanistan after the removal of the Taliban from power. However, the U.S. government soon found other targets in its "war on terror." U.S. leaders said that al-Qaeda had fled to Iraq, and that this country's leader, Saddam Hussein, had powerful and dangerous weapons at his disposal. Many leaders in the international community doubted the connection between al-Qaeda and Iraq, and the United States provided little convincing evidence. Some critics of U.S. policy suggested that American interests in Iraq had more to do with that nation's large oil reserves than with stopping terrorism. When the United States made the decision to invade Iraq, in March 2003, Canadian soldiers did not join their comrades. Though Canadian and American troops continue to work together in Afghanistan, the United States faced its war in Iraq alone. To date, more than 4,000 U.S. soldiers and as many as one million Iraqi civilians have been killed in that war.

Standing Alone

2001
The U.S.–Canada border is on high alert after terrorists strike New York City on September 11.

2002
Canada cautions citizens of Middle Eastern descent about travel to the United States.

No Missiles Here

2000s

No Missiles Here

In the early 2000s, U.S. president George W. Bush was pushing hard for what he called a "missile shield." This was a defence system intended to shoot down incoming nuclear warheads. The United States requested Canadian help, hoping to place missile defence stations in the Canadian Arctic, in order to guard against missiles flying over the North Pole. Many Canadians rejected what they saw as U.S. militarism. They felt that this new, more aggressive weapons program in the United States would create international unrest and, perhaps, a new arms race among the world's major powers. Many opponents to the missile defence program quoted physicists who said that shooting down missiles was extremely difficult and unlikely to work reliably. Others were cautious about rejecting the American proposal. They thought that declining to participate might mean being shut out of U.S. defence strategies, which are important to Canada as well. Eventually, in February 2005, Foreign Affairs Minister Pierre Pettigrew announced that Canada would not be joining the United States' plan for a missile shield.

2003
The U.S. military presents Bronze Stars to 26 Canadian soldiers.

2004
A U.S. soldier seeks refuge in Canada after refusing to deploy to Iraq.

2005
Trade in live cattle under 30 months old resumes.

2003

The Beef with Beef

In May 2003, a cow on an Alberta ranch was found to have a disease called bovine spongiform encephalopathy, commonly known as BSE or "mad cow disease." BSE is a sickness in the brain of cows that breaks down their nervous systems and eventually causes death. The germ that causes BSE in cows can cause a similar disease in humans. This is especially dangerous, because, unlike many other germs, this germ cannot be destroyed by cooking the meat of the infected animal. During a BSE outbreak in Great Britain, 163 people died of the human version of the disease. After learning of the infected cow, the United States stopped importing Canadian beef. The ban was later eased slightly, but restrictions remained in place. Beef prices fell, and ranchers began to have difficulty making ends meet. Even though the risk of infection was very low, many people in Canada stopped buying beef as well, putting even more pressure on the cattle industry. When a cow becomes infected with BSE, it can take a long time before the disease begins to show signs of damage. This meant that other cows might have been infected, and no one would know how far the disease had spread for a very long time. In December 2003, an infected cow was found in Washington state, and Canada stopped accepting imports of U.S. beef. For a long time, neither country traded beef to the other. However, in 2005, governments and ranchers began to feel more secure about the safety of North American beef, and trade resumed in full.

The Beef with Beef

2006
Canadian, U.S., British, and Iraqi soldiers rescue three hostages held in Iraq.

2007
The Canadian government teams up with U.S. millionaire Bill Gates to fight AIDS.

2006

Timber Trouble

For more than 20 years, Canada and the United States have debated what to do with softwood lumber prices. Softwood is a type of wood, often from pine trees, that is easy to work with. It forms the bulk of wood used in construction around the world. Softwood grows abundantly in Canada's forests, especially in British Columbia, on land owned mostly by the government. The government charges a relatively low price for this wood, so Canadian lumber companies can afford to sell the wood more cheaply than their U.S. competitors. For a long time, the United States had been charging duties on imports of Canadian softwood in order to allow U.S. softwood companies to compete. There were many heated discussions and negotiations about softwood lumber prices. Many Canadian companies felt that additional charges on their lumber were unfair. They wanted to continue to sell their wood at a competitive price. After much back-and-forth debate, a tentative agreement was reached in 2006. The United States agreed not to impose extra duties or taxes on Canadian softwood so long as the wood remained above a certain price. It was hoped this would allow Canadian lumber companies to continue to operate competitively in the United States and not push U.S. companies out of business. As part of the deal, the United States also returned more than $5 billion in duties it had already collected.

Timber Trouble

Into the Future

Many people across the world have disagreements. Even those with good relationships, such as Canada and the United States are some times at odds. However, these two nations are committed to resolving issues that may arise through discussion and compromise. Think about times in your own life where this sort of diplomacy could help you deal with others.

2008
GM closes a truck plant in Oshawa, costing hundreds of Canadian jobs.

2009

2010

Canada and the United States
1990s

1990s

The Royal Canadian Mickey Mouse Police

What does Mickey Mouse have to do with one of Canada's most famous symbols? In 1995, The Mounted Police Foundation contracted The Walt Disney Company Canada to market the RCMP image. Disney managed the Canadian manufacturers, who were licensed to produce consumer goods using the RCMP image—no rights were transferred, and no control was lost. Critics called the agreement a sellout of Canadian culture. Jokes about the RCMP being a "Mickey Mouse operation" were everywhere. Three years later, the fuss died down, and most critics were quiet. "The way it used to be, there were trinkets and treasures from all four corners of the world of varying quality. Now it's all high-quality, Canadian-made products: Now we get **royalties**," explained Staff Sgt. Ken Maclean. The royalties are used for a good cause. Since the beginning of the agreement, hundreds of thousands of dollars have been invested in RCMP community programs. The programs help crime prevention, drug awareness, youth education, and senior citizen support.

The Royal Canadian Mickey Mouse Police

1991
Canadian director James Cameron releases the film *Terminator 2*.

1992
For the first time, a non-U.S. team, the Toronto Blue Jays, wins the World Series Championship.

1993

Pacific Salmon

When the Pacific Salmon Treaty between Canada and the United States ended in 1993, it began a war of words. The treaty had required that fishers from each country catch only the number of fish that spawned in their own country's water. After the treaty ended, Canadian fishers claimed that the Americans were catching many more fish than their share. Fishers protested by blocking important water routes near Vancouver with their boats. Discussions for a new treaty did not go well. At one point, Canadian negotiators called an end to the talks. Tension grew when British Columbia Premier Glen Clark got involved. Clark announced that he would cancel a U.S. navy lease to an area off Vancouver Island. Federal politicians on both sides of the border stepped in to help talks begin again.

Pacific Salmon

1993
American Gary Bettman becomes commissioner of the NHL.

1994
The North American Free Trade Agreement (NAFTA) comes into effect.

1995
U.S. President Bill Clinton addresses Parliament.

1997

Saving Canadian Magazines

Canadians like reading stories about Canada. They want to know about Canadian athletes, heroes, writers, actors, accomplishments, and events. Every month Canadians prove this. Canadian magazines sell better than American magazines, even though American magazines cover 80 percent of the space at newsstands. However magazines depend on advertisements to stay in business. In 1997, the World Trade Organization ruled that Canadian tax laws were unfair to American magazine publishers. They said Canada would have to find another way to protect its magazine industry. Canadian publishers worried they would go out of business without protection. Without extra taxes, American magazines could sell advertising cheaper than Canadian magazines. If this happened, Canadian publications might lose important revenue to the Americans. In 1998, the federal government solved the problem. They passed a law to stop foreign publishers from selling advertising services in Canada.

Saving Canadian Magazines

1996
The Winnipeg Jets move south, becoming the Phoenix Coyotes.

1997
Canadian film director Atom Egoyan is nominated for the Best Director Oscar.

1998
U.S. tariffs are placed on Canadian softwood lumber.

CanCon
Nelly Furtado

1998

CanCon

What is CanCon? A Mexican holiday resort? A French cabaret dance? CanCon stands for Canadian content, which all radio stations in Canada must provide. The Canadian Radio-television and Telecommunications Commission (CRTC) is a federal government organization. It regulates how much Canadian music you hear on the radio. The CRTC wants to give Canadian musicians a chance to compete against American artists. In 1998, the CRTC raised levels of CanCon from 25 percent to 35 percent. This means that from 6 a.m. to 6 p.m. on weekdays, at least 35 percent of the music played by radio stations must be Canadian. Canadian music is defined by the CRTC as music written or performed by a Canadian, or music recorded in Canada. Many people objected to the change. They argued that most stations would not play a greater variety of Canadian bands. They would just play the same bands more times.

Into the Future

The United States has ten times Canada's population and much more money to spend. Canadians sometimes worry that uniquely Canadian things will be "drowned out" by a greater volume of U.S. culture. Think about things that are important to you that cannot be found outside of Canada. How important is it to you to preserve these things?

1999
U.S. oil company Chevron announces a major petroleum find in the Northwest Territories.

2000
Astronaut Marc Garneau, the first Canadian in space, returns to space on a NASA mission.

Canada and the United States
1980s

Cruise Missiles

1980s
Cruise Missiles

In the early 1980s, the Canadian government allowed the American government to test cruise missiles over Canada. Cruise missiles are used to carry nuclear weapons. Many Canadians did not agree with the U.S. being allowed to fly these weapons over Canada. They did not want Canada to be a part of the nuclear arms race. Some people felt it would ruin Canada's reputation as a peacekeeping nation. In 1985, a group of organizations took the Canadian government to court over cruise missiles. They argued that the missiles increased the chances of a nuclear war. The Supreme Court of Canada rejected this argument.

1980s
Acid Rain

Rain falling from the sky usually looks clean and pure. Often, rain can carry invisible pollution. When the pollution makes rain more acidic, it becomes acid rain. Acid rain can damage paint and metal. It wears away statues and buildings made of stone. The environment is especially hurt by acid rain. Acid rain changes the balance of the environment. It kills plants and fish and can affect human health. Acid rain became a serious problem for Canada during the 1980s. Acid

1981	1982	1983
The Canadarm is first used on a NASA shuttle mission.	The Canada Act, 1982 is passed.	Canada converts to the metric system, while the U.S. continues to use imperial.

rain happens when pollution in the air comes to Earth as rain. Canada tried to work out an acid rain agreement with the United States. Much of the acid rain in Canada comes from pollution just south of the border. In 1982, the U.S. refused to set any goals to reduce acid rain. The Americans criticized Canada for making negative films about acid rain. Throughout the decade, the two countries continued to argue about environmental issues.

1982

Control of the Arctic

The land in the northern Arctic belongs to Canada. Canada has had many arguments with the United States over who has control, or sovereignty, of the water in the area. Canada has little power to prevent other countries from entering the area. In 1982, a Law of the Sea Conference ruled that Canada had rights over its Arctic area. Canada claimed that it owned the area called the Northwest Passage. The Northwest Passage is a very important waterway, as it is the shortest route between the United States and Russia. The area is also a wealthy resource for oil, gas, and minerals. The United States did not agree that Canada owned this area. In 1985, the U.S. sent an **icebreaker**, the *Polar Sea*, through the Northwest Passage without permission from the Canadian government. Many Canadians were angry that the government did not prevent the icebreaker from entering Canadian waters. The Canadian government said it would be more careful about defending its territory.

Acid Rain

Control of the Arctic

1984

Canadian-American author William Gibson releases *Neuromancer*, reviving the science-fiction genre.

1985

A Royal Commission report recommends free trade with the United States.

Shamrock Summit

1985

Shamrock Summit

Canada and the United States have often disagreed about many political topics. In 1985, Prime Minister Mulroney and U.S. President Ronald Reagan held a friendly meeting called the Shamrock Summit. The summit was so named because both men have Irish ancestry. At the summit, Prime Minister Mulroney and President Reagan agreed on several military defence programs, including the Strategic Defense Initiatives (Star Wars). The two also signed the North American Air Defense Modernization agreement. This agreement updated Canada's DEW (Distant Early Warning) system that protected northern Canada and Alaska from being attacked by other nations. Another major topic of discussion was free trade between the countries. This meeting eventually led to the free trade agreement.

1986

Canadian director David Cronenberg releases the movie *The Fly* to great U.S. success.

1987

Negotiations for the Canadian-American Free Trade Agreement are successful.

Free Trade

1986

Free Trade

In 1986, Canada and the United States worked on an agreement that would allow easier trading of goods and services between the two countries. Already, Canada and the U.S. were important trading partners. Free trade was supposed to help the economies of both countries. Free trade meant that Canada could sell its resources and other goods to the U.S. market without as many taxes or restrictions. Many Canadians were against free trade with the U.S. They felt that it would mean fewer jobs for Canadians and more dependence on the U.S. With Canada being a smaller market and workforce, many people thought that jobs would go to the United States, where more labour could be found at less cost. Others were anxious to get rid of the taxes and duties paid when goods were brought across the border. The free trade agreement came into effect on January 1, 1989.

Into the Future

Canada and the United States had very different approaches to military action in the late 20th century. While the United States regularly intervened directly, Canadian troops often took peacekeeping roles or joined forces with United Nations troops. Which strategy do you think is more effective?

1988
Wayne Gretzky is traded from the Edmonton Oilers to the L.A. Kings.

1989
Canadian Sidney Altman and Thomas Chech of the U.S. share the Nobel Prize in chemistry.

1990
Canadian military join the U.S. in the Gulf War.

Canada and the United States
1970s

1970s
Not Into NATO

After reviewing Canada's foreign policy in 1969, Prime Minister Trudeau decided to decrease his involvement in NATO (North Atlantic Treaty Organization) because of the high cost of weapons, the superpowers' discussions without consulting Canada, and the reduced threat to Europe because of the growing tension between the **Soviet Union** and China. This caused conflict among Canada and the United States and many European NATO members. To maintain economic ties with European members, Trudeau reluctantly supplied arms to NATO rather than troops. In 1975, the government changed its attitude and agreed that the first priority in Western defence was Europe, but the number of Canadian troops in Europe was lower than the alliance wanted.

1971
Hurricane Beth rages along the eastern seaboard of Canada and the United States.

1972
Canada bans cigarette advertising.

1973
The OPEC embargo is harmful to most of North America.

Independent Country, Sort Of

1970
Independent Country, Sort Of

The Committee for an Independent Canada (CIC) was set up to promote cultural and economic independence from the United States and other foreign countries. It was started on September 17, 1970, and by June 1971, the committee had collected 170,000 signatures on a petition. The committee asked Prime Minister Trudeau to reduce foreign ownership and investment in Canada. Many of the committee's demands became a reality, including Petro-Canada, the Canadian Development Corporation, and the Foreign Investment Review Agency. The CIC disbanded in 1981 as it had achieved its major goals.

1974
Canada demands that its territorial waters be extended 200 kilometres from shore.

1975
The U.S. comedy show *Saturday Night Live* premieres, with a Canadian producer and actors.

Keeping the Great Lakes Great

1971

Keeping the Great Lakes Great

Talks between the United States and Canadian governments regarding the Great Lakes took place in May 1971. Both countries were concerned about pollution in the area, which affected the quality of water in the lakes. They feared that, if the situation was not addressed, people's health and property could be harmed. Protecting the Great Lakes from pollution was a joint responsibility, as both countries had rights to the water. With the population growing around the lakes on both sides of the border, the Great Lakes had begun to deteriorate. The governments agreed to develop and put to work co-operative programs to stop the problem before it escalated.

1972

Anyone But the Americans….

The Vietnam War made Canadians distrust their southern neighbours. In 1972, Prime Minister Trudeau tried to make Canada less dependent on the United States and to strengthen Canadian culture, economy, and institutions. Trudeau pursued other trading partners in Europe to replace the United States. The policy failed, but Trudeau continued his nationalistic opinions throughout his career. He openly criticized the United States's foreign and defence policies in the late seventies and early eighties.

Anyone But the Americans….

1976

The Man Who Skiied Down Everest becomes the first Canadian film to win an Oscar.

1977

The first Major League Baseball game is played between a Canadian team and an American Team.

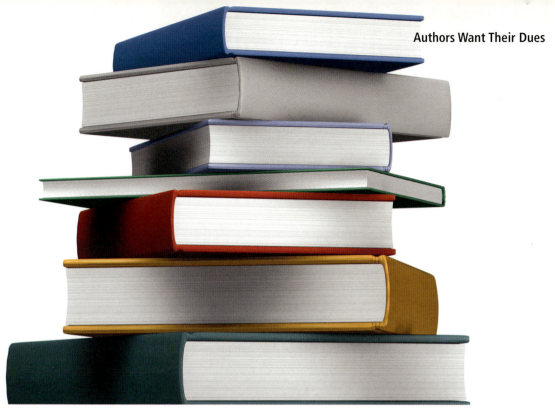

Authors Want Their Dues

1975

Authors Want Their Dues

Canadian writers took to the streets in protest on October 25, 1975. A number of well-known Canadian authors, including Pierre Berton, W.O. Mitchell, and Margaret Laurence, gathered in front of a Coles bookstore in Ottawa to protest how the major chain did business. The authors claimed that Coles sold American editions of their books at lower prices than other bookstores. Neither the authors nor the publishers received any royalties or profit from the sale of these editions. The authors refused to do book signings at Coles and asked for support in a boycott. "If Coles is going to spit in the face of Canadian writers and publishers, let's spit right back." said author Sydney Gordon.

Into the Future

Canada and the United States have many common resources along the border, such as forests and freshwater reserves. It is important to share these fairly, because overuse could damage these natural resources permanently. Which do you think is more important, short-term, rapid gain from these resources, or slower, long-term gain, that preserves them for future use?

1978
Canada begins buying new airplanes and military gear.

1979
Canadians Chris Haney and Scott Abbott invent Trivial Pursuit.

1980
Canada's National Film Board wins an Oscar for its animated films.

Canada and the United States
1960s

1960s

Anti-war Protests

By the late 1960s, the Americans had half a million troops in Vietnam, and the death toll was 33,000 and climbing. Canada was never officially involved in the war, though it did serve on a truce commission and provided medical supplies. Many Canadians opposed the war. They were upset that hundreds of Canadian firms sold war supplies to the United States and that American bomber pilots practised flying over the Canadian Prairies. As the war went on, there were several protests outside the American Embassy in Ottawa. Some of the noisiest protests occurred on university campuses. At the University of Toronto, picketers tried to evict recruiters for Dow Chemicals, producers of a chemical called napalm used in fire-bombs, during an interview session. The most effective protest came from popular singers, including Bruce Cockburn, Neil Young, and Joni Mitchell, who wrote and sang anti-war songs. In 1965, the Canadian government openly opposed the war. When Prime Minister Pearson was invited to speak at Temple University in Philadelphia, he asked for a pause in the bombing. That pause, he said, might provide an opportunity for both sides to begin peace negotiations. The next day, President Johnson grabbed Pearson by the lapels of his coat and snarled that he did not like it when Canadians came into his country and spoke against his views. Not all Canadians opposed the war. Between 12,000 and 40,000 Canadians served in the U.S. military in Vietnam, and about 100 were killed in action.

Anti-war Protests

1961
The first BOMARC missile squadron, a joint defence strategy between the U.S. and Canada, is formed.

1962
The U.S. announces a blockade of Cuba without consulting NORAD ally Canada.

Diefenbaker and Kennedy

1961

Diefenbaker and Kennedy

When President John F. Kennedy and his wife visited Ottawa on May 16, 1961, huge crowds waving Canadian and American flags lined the streets, but relations between Kennedy and Prime Minister Diefenbaker were tense. Soon after Diefenbaker was elected, he agreed to a joint air-defense plan with the United States. Then, he refused to load nuclear warheads on the missiles he had bought. In October 1962, when the world seemed to be on the brink of war during the Cuban Missile Crisis, Diefenbaker did not immediately put the Canadian military on high alert. Kennedy was furious and publicly accused Diefenbaker of not carrying out his commitments. Relations between the Canadian and American heads of state had never sunk so low. All through the winter election campaign of 1963, Diefenbaker accused the Americans of interfering in Canadian affairs. "It's me against the Americans," he said in his speeches, "fighting for the little guy." When he lost the election, he blamed Kennedy. He was disgusted when his successor, Lester Pearson, had a friendly visit with Kennedy soon after the election. The new prime minister agreed to arm Canadian missiles and fighter-bombers with atomic weapons. The Canadian people did not share Diefenbaker's dislike for Kennedy. In a poll taken on December 26, 1962, they ranked Kennedy as the person they admired most in the world. John Diefenbaker came in fifth.

1963
Diefenbaker refuses to accept U.S. nuclear weapons in Canada.

1964
Canadian nationalists oppose the Columbia River Treaty.

1965
Nearly 57 percent of Canadian exports are sold in the U.S.

1961

Squabbles over Columbia River Treaty

It took fifteen years of planning and one year of intense negotiations between Canada and the United States. Finally, on January 17, 1961, Prime Minister John Diefenbaker and President Dwight Eisenhower signed the Columbia River Treaty. The Columbia River rises in the interior of British Columbia and flows across Washington State to the Pacific Ocean. The treaty was designed for producing hydroelectric power and flood control. Canada agreed to build three giant storage dams in southern British Columbia at a cost of U.S. $345 million. The United States agreed to build the power-generating stations and to pay Canada U.S. $64 million. Both countries would share the power. British Columbia Premier W.A.C. Bennett was not satisfied with the treaty. He wanted to sell Canada's share of the power back to the Americans. So, the treaty did not come into effect until September 16, 1964. Finally, Prime Minister Pearson and President Kennedy changed the treaty after a compromise was reached: British Columbia would sell the power to the Americans for thirty years for U.S. $254 million, and then the agreement would be reconsidered.

Squabbles over Columbia River Treaty

1966
The Montreal Canadiens win the Stanley Cup over the Detroit Red Wings.

1967
Director Norman Jewison releases his film *In the Heat of the Night*, which is set and released in the United States.

Free Trade in Cars

1965

Free Trade in Cars

When Prime Minister Pearson visited President L.B. Johnson at his ranch in Texas in January 1965, he signed the Canada-U.S. Auto Pact. The agreement got rid of the heavy taxes on vehicles and parts in both countries. It created a single North American market for cars, trucks, buses, tires, and automobile parts. Either government could cancel the pact with twelve months' notice. Pearson said he expected the agreement to boost the auto industry in Canada by 25 percent and to add 50,000 new jobs. The balance of payments between the two countries would also improve for Canada. He thought consumers would be happy since the price of vehicles would fall. Pearson even hinted that free trade might be extended to other industries. "We will certainly be anxious to have a look at the other situations," he said. Critics pointed out that under the Auto Pact, Canada would never develop an independent auto industry. The giant American auto makers would own the plants, do the research and development, and Canada would continue to make parts and assemble cars.

Into the Future

Sometimes, nations that have good working relationships face times of disagreement and conflict. Still, they work together to achieve common goals. Similarly, good friends may sometimes have different opinions about an issue. Think of a time when you and a friend disagreed about something. How did you work together to resolve this disagreement?

1968
Canadian premiers debate constitutional reform.

1969
Canada criticizes the United States' role in the Vietnam conflict.

1970
Canada's population is about 21 million, compared to 203 million in the U.S.

Canada and the United States
1950s

How Wide is the Border?

1950s

How Wide is the Border?

In the 1950s, it sometimes seemed as though there was no border between the United States and Canada at all. Movies, television shows, books, music, fashions, ideas, hockey stars, and many other products moved north across the border easily. The American movies *High Noon* and *On the Waterfront* were especially popular in Canada in the 1950s. Favourite film stars included James Dean, Grace Kelly, Marilyn Monroe, and Humphrey Bogart. Popular music ranged from cowboy songs to **cool jazz**. American musicals, such as *Guys and Dolls*, were also popular with Canadians. As for sports, Americans played on Canadian teams, and Canadians played on American teams. American tourists flocked into Canada, eager to enjoy such attractions as the Stratford Festival and the National Ballet. American money also flowed across the border. This was partly because of the recent discovery of oil, uranium, and other resources in Canada. It was expensive to develop these resources, and Americans were eager to invest their money. Both countries benefited from the arrangement. But in the mid-1950s, a government report showed that Americans owned a large proportion of Canadian businesses. This worried many people. They said that Canada was turning into an American state.

1951
Canada and the United States build an expensive net of radar detectors in the Canadian North.

1952
Lester B. Pearson is elected president of the United Nations General Assembly.

Niagara Agreement

1950

Niagara Agreement

In 1950, Canada and the United States signed an agreement about the water flowing over Niagara Falls. It was called the Niagara Diversion Treaty. Both nations used the Falls to produce electricity. For both nations, Niagara Falls was also an important tourist attraction. The treaty made sure that a certain amount of water would stay in the river and continue to flow over the falls. The remainder was to be divided equally between Canada and the United States. Canada's water was diverted from the Niagara River above the falls and channelled into electric-generating stations.

1953
The Korean war ends, and Canadian and American troops head home.

1954
Construction begins on the St. Lawrence Seaway.

1955
The United States and Canada first agree to build the DEW Line.

1957
DEW Line Completed

The Distant Early Warning (DEW) Line came into operation on July 31, 1957. The DEW Line is a network of radar stations in the North. It was the result of an agreement signed between Canada and the United States in 1955. The Americans were worried that Soviet bombers might launch a surprise attack by flying over the North Pole. In order to have plenty of warning of such an attack, they needed a chain of radar stations across the Arctic—across the Canadian Arctic as well as Alaska. The DEW Line stations stretched from Alaska to Baffin Island. Although the DEW Line protected Canada as well as the United States, some Canadians were not happy about the project. They pointed out that the radar stations were American military bases. Canadians could not enter them without permission. With the stations, they claimed, Americans had taken control of large tracts of the Canadian Arctic.

1956
Leonard Cohen publishes his first book of poetry, launching his career on both sides of the border.

1957
U.S. interests control 70% of Canada's oil industry.

1957

Joint Defense Agreement

In 1958, Canada and the United States signed an agreement to create a joint force to protect North America. It was called the North American Air Defense Command (NORAD). The new defence force had its headquarters in Colorado Springs, Colorado, and was commanded by an American. His second-in-command was a senior officer in the Royal Canadian Air Force. It was agreed that NORAD would have about 200,000 soldiers, 17,000 of whom would be Canadians.

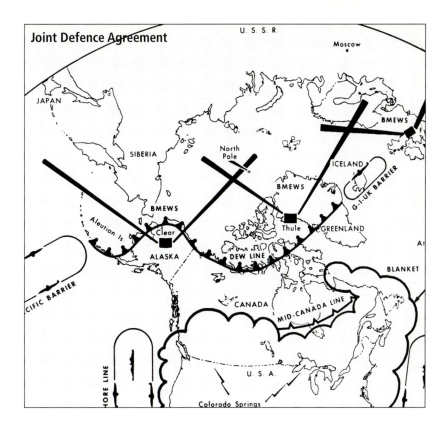

Into the Future

In the 1950s, North Americans worried about the potential expansion of the Soviet Union. Canada and the United States joined forces in many ways for their shared protection from threats, such as spies and missiles. Do you think it is important to have a strong shared defence today?

1958
Canadian singer Paul Anka is popular across North America.

1959
U.S. President Eisenhower and Queen Elizabeth open the St. Lawrence Seaway.

1960
Gordie Howe becomes the leading scorer in NHL history.

Canada and the United States
1940s

North American Defence

1940

North American Defence

In 1938, the world was bracing for an international conflict. American President Franklin D. Roosevelt promised to protect Canada if it was threatened during a war. In 1940, after two days of negotiations, the Ogdensburg Agreement was reached. It created a Permanent Joint Board of Defence for North America. It addressed issues such as delivering weapons from American factories to Canadian forces. The agreement also rested on a free exchange of defence information. If Germany or Japan attacked North America, the agreement stated that both sides would defend the coasts and make use of airfields. This agreement signalled a shift in Canada's alliance. Canada realized a common interest in ideals and geography that it shared with the United States. This commonality was no longer present with Great Britain.

1941

Hyde Park Agreement

Before the United States officially joined the war, Canada had already begun expanding its industries. It bought a great deal of equipment and machinery from the U.S. By 1941, Canada was running low on its exchange reserves of American money. This could cause major economic problems for Canada. It turned

---

1941
Canada provides secure harbour for the U.S. and Great Britain to sign the Atlantic Charter.

1942
A Japanese submarine shells Estevan Point in British Columbia.

to the United States for help. Prime Minister King and President Roosevelt came to the Hyde Park Agreement later that year. This agreement allowed for greater U.S. purchases in Canada, and for Britain to use military supplies imported into Canada from the U.S. These conditions eased the cash problem Canada was experiencing and upped Canada's holdings of American currency. Canada could now cover its imports from the United States. Any agreement bonding the U.S. and Canada was highly supported by Canadians.

1941

American Heroes

The United States joined the war in 1941. Canadians admired the strength of their southern neighbours, and polls showed that many Canadians would have liked to join the U.S. This new feeling toward the Americans worried Prime Minister King. Despite King's feelings, Canada kept a close relationship with the United States. It even expanded its defence and other relations with the United States after the war. The two countries went on to sign many agreements that aimed at securing North American borders. This was more important because of the Cold War building between the United States and the Soviet Union. These pacts included NORAD, which was a joint air defence pact signed in 1958.

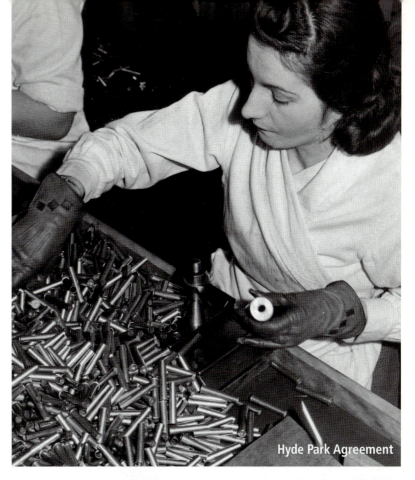

Hyde Park Agreement

American Heroes

1943
Canadian troops aid Allied forces in the invasion of Sicily.

1944
Canada appoints its first ambassador to the United States.

1945
World War II ends.

Protective Highway

1942

Protective Highway

Canada and the United States feared a Japanese attack after the bombing of Pearl Harbor in 1941. They decided to be prepared if their fears came true. In 1942, they began to build the Alaska Highway. The road spanned from Dawson Creek, British Columbia, to Fairbanks, Alaska—a total of 2,451 kilometres. A road was blasted through forests and mountains in only eight months. Crews laid up to 13 kilometres of road each day. The highway was rough. The following year, it was made a permanent, gravel-surfaced highway that could survive the temperatures in the region. Getting the highway built took the cooperation of 11,000 soldiers and 16,000 civilians. The U.S. put in $147.8 million in labour and materials. Canada gave the right-of-way and took over production of the road from Dawson Creek to the Alaska border. Canada gave the United States $108 million to pay for important components, including airfields, airstrips, and telephone systems. It did not pay for the construction itself. In 1947, the Alaska Highway was opened to the public.

1945

Brothers in Arms

The American and Canadian forces came together during the Rhineland Campaign in February 1945. The Canadian army attacked from the south, and the Americans pushed in from the north. The two came together in the area around the Rhine, a river in Germany. The mission was not easy, but together, the North Americans were successful. They were assisted by British forces as they cleared the Germans away from their last strong line of defence. This victory led to the final campaign in northwest Europe. It took the Allied forces across the Rhine and farther into Germany. The cooperation between the United States and Canada, along with the rest of the Allied forces, helped bring the war to an end.

Brothers in Arms

1946
The Canadian Citizenship Act 1946 is passed.

1947
Oil is found near Leduc, Alberta.

1948
Prime Minister King becomes suspicious of U.S. control of North America and stalls free trade talks.

The Atomic Age

1945

The Atomic Age

Prime Minister King and American President Harry Truman joined forces with Britain's Prime Minister Clement Attlee in 1945. They met in Washington, D.C., to discuss what to do about atomic weapons. The three countries were considered the atomic powers, as they were the main participants in dropping the atomic bomb on Japan. The leaders agreed to share their knowledge of atomic power, but there were concerns and conditions. They would talk about atomic weapons as long as the other countries guaranteed that such weapons would not be used in war. King, Truman, and Attlee all agreed that, if countries developed atomic weapons, it would be extremely dangerous for everyone. The leaders hoped that nations would obey the international laws and avoid war in the future. They also encouraged countries to support the new United Nations organization.

Into the Future

Many nations banded together to fight Hitler's Axis during World War II, but the bond was especially close between Canadian and U.S. soldiers. They fought many battles together, and both were known for their bravery. In what ways can you see cooperation between Canada and the United States today?

1949
Canada and the U.S. become charter members of NATO.

1950
Canada joins the Colombo Plan with the U.S. to aid the development of Asia-Pacific countries.

Canada and the United States 1930s

1930s

American Influence in Sport

Hard times resulted in the National Hockey League (NHL) becoming more American. Some teams **folded**, and other clubs moved to larger cities.

Following the collapse of the Montreal Maroons, a sports writer wrote, "[I hope] that the National Hockey League will build for the future to assure that Canadian teams will continue in what is the major domain of our great winter pastime." There were similar problems in football. The name "rugby" was replaced by "rugby football," and "touchdown" was now used instead of the word "try." It was a pity, some people said, "to see us imitate Americans." Sports writer Leslie Roberts protested that Canadians were "taking our cues from our cousins beyond the border, reconstructing our major games to appeal to the watcher rather than the players—because these games have become specialized branches of Big Business."

American Influence in Sport

1931
Canada gains the right to make policy decisions independent of Great Britain.

1932
Canada's hockey team defeats their U.S. rivals to win gold at the Winter Olympics.

1930s

Trade Across the Border

It was a long time coming, and the trade deal caused a great deal of dispute between the representatives of the two countries during the late 1930s. Prime Minister Mackenzie King and United States President Franklin Roosevelt finally signed the trade agreement. The treaty was intended to make trade across the border easier. It allowed Canadian farmers, lumber sellers, and fishermen to make more money from American sales. The import and export taxes were reduced. It would now cost Canadians less money to sell in the American market.

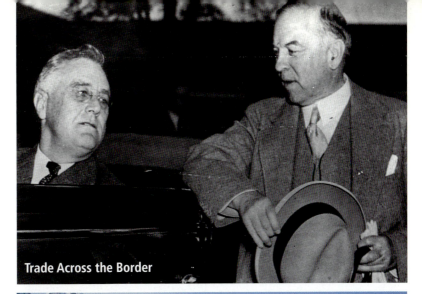

Trade Across the Border

1930s

The "Great Woods"

In Hollywood's eyes, Canada was a snowswept "Great Woods." Movies with Canadian themes, including *Men of the North*, *Mounted Fury*, *Klondike*, *Sign of the Wolf*, and *On the Great White Trail* flooded movie theatres. Why did Hollywood set so many of its films in Canada? To many Americans, Canada sounded exotic—wild and **primitive**, slightly dangerous, and scenic. Canadians were shown as simple, unsophisticated people. Moviegoers flocked to exciting, romantic films about the "Great Woods of the North." The films were about Canada and Canadian themes, but the majority of these movies were filmed in the United States. Regardless, Hollywood had discovered a winning and profitable formula that movie producers used again and again. About half of the movies made about Canada featured a Mountie (or Mounties) in the plot. Hollywood's Mountie character was courteous, kind, brave, trustworthy, and almost always got his man. He usually got his girl, too!

The "Great Woods"

1933
Franklin Roosevelt begins working toward the Canadian-American Security Alliance.

1934
The Bank of Canada is established.

1935
The Canada–United States Trade Agreement is signed.

1930s

Canada-U.S. Trade Relations Improve

In 1930, Canada and the United States began a tariff war. The Americans passed the Hawley-Smoot Tariff, which increased the duty paid on imports. Tariffs reached the highest levels in history. Canada reacted by raising its own tariffs. Prime Minister Bennett promised Canadians that he would charge into international markets and decrease Canada's dependence on the United States. In 1932, Bennett hosted the Imperial Economic Conference in Ottawa. It worked to encourage trade and change the tariff system within the British Commonwealth. By 1934, trade between the two countries began to improve. After the United States passed the Reciprocal Trade Agreements, the two governments met to figure out the best way to lower tariffs and increase trade. In 1935, Prime Minister King finished off the trade agreement started by Bennett. A second and more far-reaching agreement was entered into in 1938. This led to tariffs between Canada and the United States being reduced even further. This cooperation and acceptable trade relations helped both countries during the onset of World War II.

Canada-U.S. Trade Relations Improve

1936
The first rodeo arena and grandstand in Mississippi are constructed by Albertan Earl Bascom.

1937
Two American climbers make the first ascent of Mount Lucania, the third-highest peak in Canada.

Owning the Airwaves

1937

Owning the Airwaves

At night, it was easier for most people in Alberta to listen to an American radio station, or even one from Mexico, than a Canadian broadcast. There were two problems. Two or more radio stations could broadcast on the same radio wave. Neither came through really clearly because they interfered with each other. An agreement between Canada and the United States in 1937 gave Canada six frequencies, and the countries shared 24 others. The United States got the remaining 94 frequencies. Most American stations were at least 20 times more powerful than Canadian stations. In some rural areas of the province, 40 percent of the population could not get a Canadian station that did not have a lot of static. Whereas most privately owned stations relied on American programming, by law the CBC had to offer mostly Canadian content. In 1938, for example, the CBC had 60 and a half hours of Canadian programs, 26 hours of American, and 12 hours of overseas programs.

Into the Future

Even without the Hollywood hype, Canada has many amazing natural treasures, from the Rocky Mountains to the Bay of Fundy. American tourists who come to see these treasures are an important source of income for Canadians. Think about the features of your community that attract tourism.

1938
Franklin Roosevelt becomes the first U.S. president to visit Canada.

1939
Canada declares war on Germany.

1940
The U.S. and Canada sign the Ogdensburg Agreement on continental defence.

Canada and the United States
1920s

Brain Drain

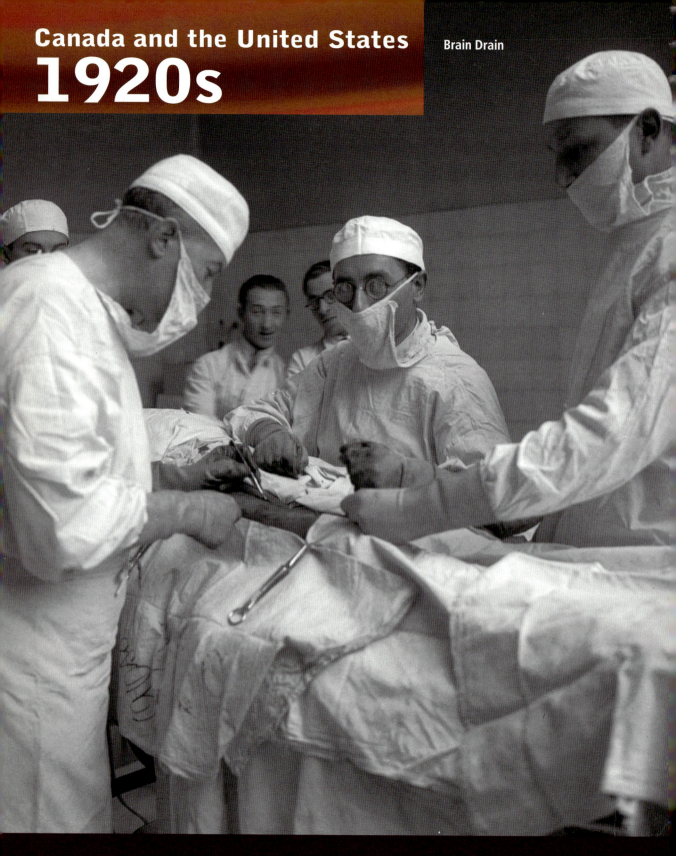

1921
Canadian exports to the United States exceed exports to Great Britain for the first time.

1922
The first documentary film, *Nanook of the North*, is released in the U.S. and Canada.

1920s

Brain Drain

More than one million Canadians left for the United States. This was where the jobs were in the 1920s. Maritimers and Quebeckers were the most likely to leave. In 1925, a Halifax newspaper complained, "there are more Nova Scotians in Massachusetts than there are in Nova Scotia." Most alarming was the large number of well-educated Canadians who left. Eleven per cent of the University of Toronto, 15 per cent of the University of Western Ontario, and 36 per cent of Acadia University graduates left for the States. The numbers were highest among medical and engineering students.

1923

Growing American Control

Canada moved slowly away from Great Britain and closer to the United States. For the first time, Canada sold more goods to the United States than to Britain in 1923. Around the same time, Canada imported two-thirds of its foreign goods from the south, and much of Canada's natural resources were owned by American-controlled companies. A similar change was happening in movies, books, radios, and newspapers. When radio frequencies were divided in 1924, Canada agreed to take six radio frequencies and have partial use of another 11 frequencies. The United States received the remainder of the 95 known frequencies. The limited range of many Canadian stations meant that some rural areas received no radio signals at all, whereas others had their signals drowned out by the more powerful American transmitters. Since the American radio stations had more people in their market, they could afford to develop better and more varied programs, including comedies and dramas. As a result, some Canadian stations obtained the right to broadcast American shows by becoming **affiliates** with such networks as CBS.

Growing American Control

Canadian vs. American spellings:

Canadian	American
labour	labor
metre	meter
colour	color
centre	center
theatre	theater

By 1930, about 80 percent of the radio programs listened to by Canadians came from the United States. Canadians also watched more American movies and read more American books and magazines than Canadian-made ones. This situation worried some people, who feared Canadians were losing their culture. *Maclean's* magazine promised to print only Canadian non-fiction writing and to use Canadian spellings. Other Canadian magazines followed suit.

1923
The Halibut Treaty is signed between Canada and the United States.

1924
The Royal Canadian Air Force is formed.

1925
The Lake of the Woods Treaty is signed.

Play for Play's Sake

1926
Canada returns its currency to the Gold Standard.

1927
The Canada Pension Act is rolled out.

1928
The New York Rangers defeat the Montreal Maroons to win the Stanley Cup.

1926

Play for Play's Sake

Women began to play sports just for the sake of playing sports. This idea led to the development of the Women's Amateur Athletic Federation in 1926. In the new organization, scores were often not recorded. It was how you played the game that mattered. Under the motto "A Sport for Every Girl, and Every Girl in a Sport," American female physical educators tried to encourage a lifetime of participation by making athletics available to everyone. They stressed enjoyment over winning, recreational sports which could be played after graduation, and playing sports just to be playing. This meant many things to sports. It brought an end to intercollegiate and interscholastic contests, and it hoped to stop the use of women in sports as novelties to sell game tickets. Educators also wanted to show that women were beautiful and strong, despite their femininity. This program employed only female coaches, administrators, and referees. As an alternative to interschool contests, girls participated in intramural games and play days. The American ideas about women in sports were soon introduced to Canadians. American journals were widely read in Canada, and many Canadian physical educators received advanced degrees in the United States. This influence was especially true in central Canada, where competition within a school became more important than competing against other schools. Canadians adopted the American idea of play for play's sake. Women were to have female referees and coaches, female rules, and separate women's organizations.

1927

Hockey Crosses the Border

In the 1920s, the National Hockey League (NHL) expanded into the United States. Before this time, nearly every team was Canadian. The Boston Bruins were the first U.S. team to join the NHL, in 1925. A year later, William Dwyer bought the Hamilton Tigers and moved the team to New York. They were called the Americans. The next year, four more American teams were added to the NHL. By 1927, the league was made up of 10 clubs: two each in New York and Montreal, and one each in Ottawa, Toronto, Detroit, Pittsburgh, Boston, and Chicago. The next year, the New York Rangers became the first American NHL team to win the championship.

Hockey Crosses the Border

Into the Future

At times, the U.S. economy is stronger than Canada's. In these times, people often move south to work and take advantage of U.S. prosperity. In recent years, some U.S. citizens have moved to Canada to be part of the booming Prairie economies. What is the trend where you live?

1929

Canada's population tops 10 million for the first time—the U.S. population stands at 120 million.

1930

R.B. Bennett defeats William Lyon Mackenzie King in the federal election.

Canada and the United States
1910s

Industrialization Brings Changes

Anti-Americanism in Canada

1910s
Industrialization Brings Changes

Industrialization in North America expanded quickly in the early part of the 20th century. American companies saw the opportunity to make a great deal of money in Canada. Hundreds of millions of American dollars flowed into Canada to set up subsidiaries and branch plants. Americans bought promising Canadian companies that would supply the fast-developing new markets—electric appliances, metal processing, and motor vehicles were attractive products to Americans. There did not seem to be anything wrong with this American influence and ownership in Canada, at least until hard times hit. Only then did Canada begin to realize the vulnerable position it was in. It had grown dependent on the United States, a condition that many prime ministers to follow would try to correct.

1910s
Being Neighbourly

Reciprocity, or the failure of it, caused a rift between Canada and the United States. Laurier pushed to pass the agreement, but Robert Borden helped **quash** it. Once Borden was voted into office, he quickly told the Americans that Canada wanted to keep a strong relationship with its neighbour. When the war hit, Canada joined the fight, and the United States remained neutral until 1917. Once both countries were fighting for the Allies, Canada and the United States realized more and more how similar their cultures and interests were. By the end of the war, Canada seemed to understand and relate to the United States better than it did to Great Britain.

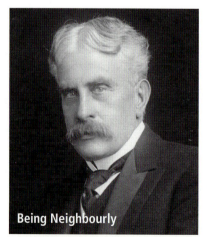
Being Neighbourly

1910s
Anti-Americanism in Canada

Many people resented Canada's growing ties with the United States. Laurier's reciprocity agreement made these feelings even stronger. People opposed to the agreement told Canadians that, if the bill was passed, Canada would lose ties to Great Britain and maybe even fall apart altogether. Clifford Sifton, an influential politician, resigned from the Cabinet. He feared that Laurier was endangering Canada's relationship with the Empire. The American Speaker of the House, James Beauchamp Clark, added fuel to the fire. He said that he looked forward to the day when the American flag was raised over every inch of British North American land, right to the North Pole. Comments like these made Canadians even more nervous about the Americans' intentions regarding free trade.

1911 — Robert Borden is elected prime minister.

1914 — Canada joins World War I.

1917 — U.S. troops join World War I.

1910

Protecting Canadian Steel

In June 1910, Max Aitken established the Steel Company of Canada (Stelco). The Quebec businessman brought together the Hamilton Steel and Iron Company with the Montreal Rolling Mills to form the new company. He also involved steel finishing companies in Quebec and Ontario. The reason for the merger was simple: Canadian businesspeople feared American domination of their markets. Aitken knew that, if the new company controlled the overall operations of steel works, it would not be as vulnerable to United States Steel. Before the establishment of Stelco, the American company did not have competition. It could bring in huge amounts of steel products or charge finishing plants in Canada large amounts of money for steel.

Protecting Canadian Steel

1911

Reciprocity

Prime Minister Wilfrid Laurier tried to convince Canadians that a trade agreement between Canada and the United States was a good idea. In 1911, he defended the International Reciprocal Trade Agreement that he was working on with American President William Taft. People feared that such a deal would mean that Canada would be dependent on the United States for a strong economy. Laurier promised Canadians that freer trade between the countries would help Canada without damaging the close ties it shared with Great Britain. The United States Senate passed the Reciprocity Bill on July 22, 1911. It voted in favour of the agreement by 25 votes. The bill became law, at least south of the border. Laurier, although a strong and convincing speaker, did not sell Canadians on free trade. He lost the federal election later that year to Robert Borden's Conservative party.

Reciprocity

1917

War Over Peace

Canada and the United States worked together when the Americans joined the war in 1917. However, when countries were preparing to talk about the terms of the peace agreement, the United States tried to keep Canada and the other dominions from participating. They argued that allowing the nations under British control to be part of the process would simply mean that Britain would have six extra seats. Americans assumed that Canada would go along with whatever Great Britain said. The United States also fought against Canada's membership to the League of Nations. The Americans wanted to deal directly with Great Britain in any matters relating to Canada. They had found that Canadians were standing up for themselves more. Great Britain would be more likely to sacrifice Canadians' interests and support American agendas. The United States finally withdrew their objections, giving Canada the right to sign the peace treaty and join the League of Nations.

War Over Peace

1918

World War I ends, with Canada and its U.S. allies having suffered great casualties.

1920

Canada is a founding member in the League of Nations, despite the U.S. not joining.

Canada and the United States
1900s

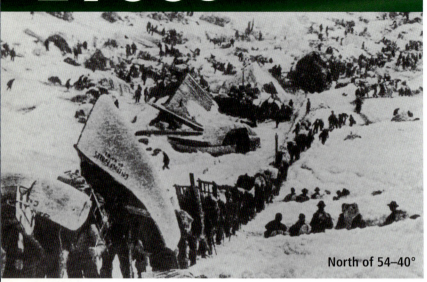
North of 54–40°

1900s
North of 54–40°

The Klondike Gold Rush of 1898 had brought many Americans into Canada's North. Alaska, which the United States had purchased from the Russians in 1867, had a long piece of coastland that was known as the Alaskan Panhandle. The boundary along this strip of land was the same as what Britain and Russia had agreed upon in 1825. However, the 1825 agreement was rather vague. It stated that the border was to run from latitude 54–40° north, following a range of mountains 16 kilometres inland and parallel to the coast. However, in some areas, no mountains existed. Canada argued that, when there were no mountains along the coastline, the offshore islands actually were the mountains. Therefore, 16 kilometres inland gave Canada rights to the coastline at those points. Canada wanted access to the heads of certain fjords, particularly Lynn Canal, which was the entry point for gold seekers into the Yukon.

The United States and Canada could not resolve the dispute. The matter was handed over to an international tribunal in 1903. There were three Americans, two Canadians, and one Briton on the tribunal. The British vote went to the Americans. Canadians felt betrayed, especially since Canada had just finished helping the British fight the Boer War.

1900s
The Last, Best West— Advertising Canada To Americans

In the United States, nearly all the free agricultural lands were gone by 1890. Clifford Sifton, Minister of the Interior, made a special effort to attract American settlers to Canada. One prospective settler wrote, "I have four sons old enough to take land. We are farming out here [in South Dakota], but land is too high in price to buy a large enough farm for myself and the boys." Canada issued millions of pamphlets describing the benefits and possibilities of living in the Canadian West. Advertisements were placed in more than 8,000 farm journals and rural newspapers.

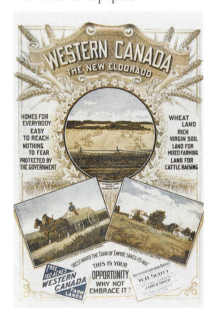

The Last, Best West—Advertising Canada To Americans

1902
Canadian troops return home after the Second Boer War ends.

1903
The Alaska Boundary dispute is settled.

1904
Ford opens Canada's first automobile plant in Windsor, Ontario.

Closed Arms

Canada Welcomes American Immigrants

1900s

Closed Arms

African Americans in Oklahoma wanted to move to the Canadian West to take advantage of the cheap, fertile land advertised by the Canadian government. However, they discovered that Canada's open-arms policy did not apply to them. There was no law against admitting African American settlers to Canada, but all restrictions respecting such issues as health and money were strictly enforced. The Canadian government officials used the excuse that African Americans were not suited to Canadian conditions and climate and stopped them from entering.

1900

Canada Welcomes American Immigrants

American settlers arrived in Canada in droves. The Canadian government welcomed these newcomers with cheap land. Americans kept rolling into the country to take advantage of the generous offer.

The campaign for settlers from the United States was a huge success. In 1900, approximately 19,000 American settlers came to Canada, and by 1905, that number had increased to 58,000. American settlers were valued because they already had knowledge of farming techniques suitable to the Prairies, they spoke English, and they frequently brought cash or equipment with them. Some Canadian newspapers called the huge number of American immigrants "The American Invasion." Most came from Iowa, Nebraska, or South Dakota and settled mainly in Alberta and Saskatchewan.

1903

Alaska Dispute

In 1903, representatives of Canada, Great Britain, and the United States discussed the boundary between Canada and Alaska. The two Canadians on the Alaska Boundary Commission would not agree to the boundary recommendations. They argued that all of the Americans' suggestions were accepted—the British wanted to please the United States, so Canada was virtually ignored. The British commissioner, Lord Alverstone, tried to bully the men into signing the deal, but Louis Jetté and A.B. Aylesworth refused. They walked away from the signing ceremony. Canada's disapproval of the agreement did not stop it from being finalized. Lord Alverstone and the American commissioners each signed the agreement. Canada was not needed to make the decision binding. The Canadian commissioners continued to protest the decision, but it did no good. The boundary was set.

Alaska Dispute

1908
The Grain Grower's Guide is first published, finding much use on both sides of the border.

1910
U.S. explorer Robert Peary claims to be the first person to reach the North Pole.

ACTIVITY
Into the future

Every day, Canadian and U.S. officials must make decisions about how to react to events taking place around the world. They must carefully look at the details of each event to determine if they should become involved. In some cases, officials disagree about the most suitable course of action. Other times, the case is very clear, and officials quickly put a plan in place.

Once Canada and the United States have determined how they will become involved in an international affair, the general public learns the details of the plan. Often, these plans receive wide support from U.S. citizens. However, some actions receive a negative response. These plans become the cause of debates, as people try to determine how the government should respond and why.

Host a Debate

When people have different opinions about a subject, they may host a debate. A debate can be used to encourage others to support a specific opinion, subject, or belief. During a debate, individuals or teams present the reasons why they support or oppose a specific subject. Once both sides have presented their cases, they can take turns defending any new points that were raised during the initial statements. In the end, the individual or team with the strongest argument is determined to be the winner of the debate.

With a group of friends, try hosting a debate about a foreign affairs subject that is currently in the news. You may choose to debate that Canada and the United States should take a different course of action with regard to this subject or that the current plan is appropriate. You may want to propose that the United States offer assistance in a new matter. The opposing team would debate why Canada and the United States should remain neutral.

FURTHER Research

Many books and websites provide information on Canada/U.S. relations. To learn more about this topic, borrow books from the library, or surf the Internet.

Books
Most libraries have computers that connect to a database for researching information. If you input a key word, you will be provided with a list of books in the library that contain information on that topic. Non-fiction books are arranged numerically, using their call number. Fiction books are organized alphabetically by the author's last name.

Websites
To learn more about Canada/U.S. relations, visit www.cbc.ca/canadaus.

For additional information about Canada/U.S. relations, surf to http://geo.international.gc.ca/can-am/main/menu-en.asp.

Glossary

affiliates: groups connected with other, similar groups

cool jazz: a style of jazz music that combines bop and swing

folded: stopped operating

icebreaker: a ship designed to break through ice

primitive: having to do with an early or first stage of development

quash: to suppress or crush

royalties: payments to authors for each copy of their books sold

Soviet Union: a former communist country in eastern Europe and northern Asia which was established in 1922 and included Russia and 14 other soviet socialist republics

Index

Alaska 16, 28, 32, 44, 45
Arctic 7, 15, 28

beef 8
border 6, 11, 15, 17, 20, 21, 26, 28, 31, 32, 34, 35, 43, 44, 45

CBC 37

defence 7, 16, 18, 20, 23, 29, 30, 31, 32, 37

free trade 11, 15, 16, 17, 25, 32, 42, 43

hockey 26, 34
Hollywood 35, 37, 39

immigrants 45

missiles 7, 14, 22, 23, 29

NATO 18, 33

RCMP 10
Russia 15, 44

salmon 11
softwood 9, 12

terrorism 6

World War I 42, 43
World War II 31, 33, 36